a new you.

your new life in Jesus

DALE A. O'SHIELDS

A New You
© *Copyright 2020 by Dale A. O'Shields*

ISBN 978-0-9898891-4-8

Printed in the United States of America

Foreword

The greatest decision any of us can make is the decision to give our heart and life to Jesus Christ. A relationship with Jesus secures our eternal destiny and leads to genuine fulfillment in this life. God's promise for our future is revealed in the words of the prophet Jeremiah:

> "For I know the plans I have for you," declares the Lord, "plans to prosper you and not to harm you, plans to give you hope and a future." Jeremiah 29:11 NIV

To discover and live out these wonderful plans God

has for us, we must take seriously our responsibility to grow in the Lord by understanding and applying His Word.

In this book I want to help you get a good start on this journey toward spiritual growth and fruitfulness. The truths addressed here are essential to establishing a foundation for a strong and enduring Christian life.

As you begin to follow God's blueprint for your life, I know you will find great joy in His purposes and experience His amazing peace along the way.

Let's get started!

*When I came to faith in Christ,
I began to learn that everything good in my
life was a gift from God, not something I
could earn or take credit for on my own.*

— Roxonne

God paved the way
for you to leave the
road of death and
enter the road of life.

Chapter 1
God's Plan

Anything that's built well begins with a plan. This is true for your life. A well-built life doesn't happen by accident. It requires a plan. Not just any plan, but the right plan.

The right plan for your life starts with God. God has an incredible, wonderful future for you. It's much better than anything you could imagine or create for yourself or anything that others could create for you.

See, God knows you. He knows you better than you know yourself. He created you! You carry a label in your soul that reads, "Designed By God." He created you for a purpose and He has a specific plan for your life.

But there's a problem. By nature we don't cooperate very well with our Designer. In fact, we have an inner urge to live life on our own. We want to choose our own way. We like to be our own boss. And without realizing it, we ignore, reject and dismiss God.

Without a personal connection with God, our life choices are directed by our wants and feelings, or by the opinions and pressures of people around us. The result is a life that misses God's best, a life that doesn't work very well, or potentially, a life that is miserable and destructive.

There's something else to remember about God's plan for your life. It actually goes beyond this life. God designed you to live forever. Yes, one day you will die. Life as you've known it in this physical world will end. But there's an inner part of you that will live forever in a real, eternal place. God wants that place to be with Him!

This brings us back to our problem—our natural tendency to ignore, reject and dismiss God. When we fail to follow God's plan now, we're also saying no to His plan for us for eternity.

God's plan is all about a personal relationship with Him now and for eternity. It's about turning from your own way, turning to God, and following Him as the true Leader of your life. It's about committing your life to Him.

The good news is that God has made this possible! He took the steps necessary to make sure that every willing person can have a personal relationship with Him and discover the plan He has for their life now and forever! This pathway to a personal relationship with God is found in the miraculous book called the Bible.

What steps do you need to take to have a personal relationship with God now and for eternity?

Admit your problem.

Yes, we all have a spiritual problem. By nature we ignore, reject and dismiss God from our lives. We disobey Him. We choose to live as if we're the boss of our lives instead of letting our Creator direct and lead us.

This is called sin. We are all sinners. We have all turned away from God when we should have turned to Him. This is our biggest problem!

> Romans 3:23 (NLT)
> For everyone has sinned; we all fall short of God's glorious standard.

No one can solve a problem until they admit the problem! This is your first step toward God.

Acknowledge the consequences.

When you choose the wrong road—the one with the "danger" sign—you end up in the wrong place and often in very bad places. The same is true when you choose the road that leads away from God rather than toward Him.

Sin brings consequences. It brings death and destruction instead of the life God intends for you.

> Romans 6:23 (NCV)
> The payment for sin is death. But God gives us the free gift of life forever in Christ Jesus our Lord.

Most people never change until they see and feel the need to change. We need to change our spiritual direction because of where sin leads us. Sin has terrible, deadly consequences.

Accept God's solution.

The good news is that God has provided the solution for your problem! He paved the way for you to leave the road of death and enter the road of life. He did this because He loves you. He offers this solution as a free gift to all who will accept it.

Romans 5:8 (NIV)
But God demonstrates His own love for us in this: While we were still sinners, Christ died for us.

John 3:16 (NIV)
For God so loved the world that he gave his one and only Son, that whoever believes in him shall not perish but have eternal life.

Jesus is the way God has provided. By dying on the cross and rising from the dead, He took the punishment we deserved and paid the price for our sins.

Now we are invited to believe in Him as our risen Lord and Savior. When we put our faith in Him, we are given a clean slate, a new start, and we're changed from the inside out. We're put on a new road—the road of life rather than the one that leads to death. This is called the gift of salvation!

Romans 10:9, 10, 13 (NLT)
If you openly declare that Jesus is Lord and believe in your heart that God raised him

God's Plan   13

from the dead, you will be saved. For it is by believing in your heart that you are made right with God, and it is by openly declaring your faith that you are saved. ... For "Everyone who calls on the name of the Lord will be saved."

So here's the question: Have you accepted God's solution? Have you received Jesus as Lord and Savior of your life? Have you put your faith in Him and stepped off the road to death on to the road of life?

If not, you can do that right now by simply talking to God. Something like the following prayer will help you receive Jesus Christ today:

Dear God, I admit that I have chosen my own way instead of Yours and sinned against You. I am a sinner. I'm so sorry for all my sins and turn away from them now to You.

I believe that Jesus is the Son of God. I believe that He died on the cross to pay for my sins. I believe that Jesus rose from the dead.

Jesus, I ask you to come into my life and take control of me. I receive you as my Lord and Savior. Thank you for forgiving me and saving me. Thank you for answering my prayer and coming into my life.

In Jesus' name. Amen.

Go forward with God.

Congratulations! When you received Jesus, you entered into God's family as one of His dear children. You are a new person with a brand new life in Him.

John 1:12 (TLB)
But to all who received him, he gave the right to become children of God. All they needed to do was to trust him to save them.

2 Corinthians 5:17 (NLT)
This means that anyone who belongs to Christ has become a new person. The old life is gone; a new life has begun.

Now it's time to move forward with Christ, taking steps of growth in your exciting new life in Him.

> Colossians 2:6, 7 (TLB)
> And now just as you trusted Christ to save you, trust him, too, for each day's problems; live in vital union with him. Let your roots grow down into him and draw up nourishment from him. See that you go on growing in the Lord, and become strong and vigorous in the truth you were taught. Let your lives overflow with joy and thanksgiving for all he has done.

I'm a new person in Jesus!
He forgave me completely and delivered
me from a very troubled past.

— Alice

*Worship allows me to express
my gratitude and complete faith in Jesus,
and frees my mind of worry and doubt.*

– Daniel

Now it's time to
move forward with
Christ, taking steps
of growth in your
exciting new life in
Him.

Chapter 2

Growing Up

Watching something grow is fun. If you've ever planted a flower seed in a cup, it's a great day when a little green shoot breaks through the soil. It's thrilling to see the seedling grow into a mature plant and eventually produce a beautiful blossom. Growth is great! It's exciting!

When we give our lives to God by personally accepting Jesus Christ, we're like a seed that has been planted in soil. God's life has come into our spirit and soul. New spiritual potential is in us. Everything needed to blossom and bear fruit is given to us. We are "good to grow!"

But growth isn't automatic. There are things that need to happen for a seed to become a healthy seedling, and eventually a mature plant with beautiful blooms. Someone must supply water, warmth, sunlight and soil nutrients if the plant is going to grow into its full potential.

The same is true for your spiritual life. If you're going to experience God's plan for your life and reach the highest and best life God designed for you, you must grow as a follower of Jesus Christ. To grow, you must make sure the right spiritual ingredients are added in your life.

The good news is that God has provided every resource you need to grow into the person He wants and designed you to be! They're available. They're simple to add. They will absolutely change your life for the better!

It's now time to start watering, warming and

feeding the life of Jesus in you. How do you do this? Here are your next steps:

Get God's Word, the Bible, inside you.

Jesus said that God's Word is life-giving food. We need it to survive and thrive.

> Matthew 4:4 (NLT)
> But Jesus told him, "… People do not live by bread alone, but by every word that comes from the mouth of God."

Simply reading the Bible every day for a few minutes is a good starting point for getting God's Word inside you. Take five or ten minutes during your day and read a Bible verse or chapter. Schedule this time regularly so it becomes a new habit. The Bible is a supernatural book that will change your life.

You may be thinking, "I don't know where to start or how to read the Bible." At first glance, reading the Bible may seem overwhelming. But God will help you understand it.

Here are a few simple suggestions that will guide
you in getting the most from your Bible:

- Get an easy to understand Bible translation,
  like the New International Version (NIV)
  or New Living Translation (NLT). You
  can get these at a Christian bookstore, an
  online bookstore, or by downloading online
  versions. A great place to find online Bibles
  is www.youversion.com.

- Ask God to help you as you read. He wrote
  the Book! The Holy Spirit will give you
  understanding. Ask!

- Begin with the book of John. Why? John
  gives us the story of Jesus in a very clear
  way. Get to know Jesus Christ verse by
  verse and chapter by chapter as you read
  through the book. After finishing John, start
  reading Matthew, Mark and Luke, and
  learn about Jesus from their stories.

  Another great thing to do is to read a Psalm
  or Proverb each day. If you're not sure

where to find these books in the Bible, use the table of contents. Before long, you'll be familiar with the way the Bible is structured.

- Find a good devotional book that will help you learn about and apply the Bible to your life. You can find these at any Christian bookstore. They're also available online. If you need help finding one, ask another strong Christian or church leader for a recommendation.

- When reading your Bible, try putting yourself into the passage. Think about the emotions of the people in the verses you're reading. This will bring the Scriptures to life and help you better see how God's Word applies to you.

- Ask questions as you read your Bible: What does it mean? What can I learn from this? What is here that will help me live for Jesus? You may want to keep a journal of what you're thinking about and learning as you're reading God's Word.

- Memorize some key verses. It's valuable to get God's commands, principles and promises into your mind and heart. They'll comfort, encourage and help you as you go through your day and as you move forward in your life.

Psalm 119:11 (NIV)
I have hidden your word in my heart that I might not sin against you.

Getting God's Word inside you is a key to your spiritual growth. Read it. Think about it. Memorize it. Feed on it every day!

Become a regular, personal worshiper of God.

To grow in your relationship with God, you'll need to learn something about worship. Worship is connecting with God through prayer and praise. Worship is remembering and expressing how great God is and how small we really are. Worship is also communicating with God about our lives. We bring our needs and concerns to Him in prayer, knowing that He hears and answers us. Worship is spending time with God.

Take some time each day to talk to God. Thank and praise Him. Prayer and praise are not complicated. Through faith in Jesus, you're God's child. He's your Heavenly Father and Friend. Share your worries with God. Ask Him for wisdom and guidance. Pray for strength. Also thank Him for His love and blessings. Remember, God is listening. You'll be amazed at how He will answer!

Matthew 6:9-13 (NIV)
This, then, is how you should pray: "Our Father in heaven, hallowed be your name, your kingdom come, your will be done, on earth as it is in heaven. Give us today our daily bread. And forgive us our debts, as we also have forgiven our debtors. And lead us not into temptation but deliver us from the evil one."

Philippians 4:6, 7 (TLB)
Don't worry about anything; instead, pray about everything; tell God your needs, and don't forget to thank him for his answers. If

you do this, you will experience God's peace, which is far more wonderful than the human mind can understand. His peace will keep your thoughts and your hearts quiet and at rest as you trust in Christ Jesus.

Learn to think and live God's way.

Our thinking affects everything we do. If you think the wrong way, you'll live the wrong way.

The world around us rarely thinks about God. Neither does the world think like God thinks. People who don't live for God have a different set of values and priorities than those who do. Since we live in the world environment, we're programmed and influenced to hold the same kind of thinking, values and priorities as the world. To grow as a follower of Jesus, you must begin to think, value and prioritize life differently. You're a new person living a new life in a new Kingdom and this requires a new way of thinking!

Here's how the Bible describes this new kind of thinking:

Philippians 4:8 (NIV)
Finally, brothers and sisters, whatever is
true, whatever is noble, whatever is right,
whatever is pure, whatever is lovely, whatever
is admirable—if anything is excellent or
praiseworthy— think about such things.

Ephesians 4:21-24 (NLT)
Since you have heard about Jesus and have
learned the truth that comes from him, throw
off your old sinful nature and your former
way of life, which is corrupted by lust and
deception. Instead, let the Spirit renew your
thoughts and attitudes. Put on your new nature,
created to be like God—truly righteous and
holy.

Ephesians 4:23, 24 (TLB)
Now your attitudes and thoughts must all be
constantly changing for the better. Yes, you
must be a new and different person, holy and
good. Clothe yourself with this new nature.

Ask God to help you think differently. Consistently
fill your mind with good, pure thoughts and your

attitudes will be more positive, your relationships will improve and your life will continue to change for the better!

Taking the steps to get God's Word inside you, to become a worshiper of God and to learn to think about life God's way pays off. You'll move forward in your relationship with Jesus and your life will start to bloom in beautiful ways.

Reading the Bible every day continually transforms my life for the better. Absorbing God's Word has empowered me to act and think according to the truth I'm taking in.

— Jack

Your life will
start to bloom in
beautiful ways.

Chapter 3

Getting Stronger

There are some other important things you can do to grow stronger as a Jesus follower.

Let's look at another example, your muscles. They're obviously an important part of your physical body. They give you agility, ability and endurance. However, your muscles will never reach their highest potential without effort, action and exercise.

You want to do everything possible to have strong spiritual muscles. Why? They will help you stand firm in your relationship with Jesus Christ. They will help you overcome the temptations that will come your way. They will help you help other people come to know Jesus as you have come to know Him.

To build strong spiritual muscles, you need to take some important steps:

Go public with your faith and get baptized.

While our relationship with God is personal, it's not private. You need to identify yourself publicly as a Jesus follower. Look at what Jesus said about this:

> Matthew 10:32, 33 (NLT)
> Everyone who acknowledges me publicly here on earth, I will also acknowledge before my Father in heaven. But everyone who denies me here on earth, I will also deny before my Father in heaven.

We publicly show our commitment to Jesus in several ways.

A first step for many is in a church service. There is no better place to acknowledge Jesus before others than in the church. This can happen when the pastor gives you an opportunity to receive Jesus during the service. Take the step! People in church will celebrate your commitment with you.

We should also communicate our commitment to Jesus Christ to family and friends. In your day-to-day relationships, let people know you are a follower of Jesus. Don't be ashamed or afraid!

There will be different responses when you share your faith with others. Some will be excited about your experience. Others may be happy for you but not interested for themselves. There may be some that will not understand or support this new step in your life. They may even be hostile about it.

No matter how others respond, always be gracious, patient and prayerful. Don't let anyone's response to your faith shake your faith. Stay strong.

Water baptism is another important way we publicly declare our faith in Christ. Jesus Himself was baptized giving us an example to follow:

> Matthew 3:13-17 (NLT)
> Then Jesus went from Galilee to the Jordan River to be baptized by John. But John tried to talk him out of it. "I am the one who needs to be baptized by you," he said, "so why are you coming to me?" But Jesus said, "It should be done, for we must carry out all that God requires." So John agreed to baptize him. After his baptism, as Jesus came up out of the water, the heavens were opened and he saw the Spirit of God descending like a dove and settling on him. And a voice from heaven said, "This is my dearly loved Son, who brings me great joy."

Jesus commanded His followers to be baptized, to show the world that they truly were His followers:

> Matthew 28:19, 20 (NLT)
> Therefore, go and make disciples of all the nations, baptizing them in the name of the Father and the Son and the Holy Spirit. Teach

these new disciples to obey all the commands I have given you. And be sure of this: I am with you always, even to the end of the age.

When someone is baptized they are taken down into water and brought back up from the water. This symbolizes to everyone watching your commitment to Jesus—dying to your old way of living and rising up from the water to live a new life in Jesus Christ!

If you have not been baptized since you invited Jesus into your life, do this as soon as possible. Get baptized and show your family and friends that you are serious about your faith in Jesus Christ!

Make wise decisions about the people in your inner circle of friends.

Becoming a follower of Jesus means that you now want to live His way. This makes you stand out from the crowd around you.

As a Jesus follower, it's important to make wise choices about who you allow to influence you.

Certainly you are called to love everyone. You want to influence everyone you can to experience God's love. But who you allow to influence you is a different story.

The people in your inner circle of friends impact your life greatly. They'll lift you up or drag you down. They'll help you in your relationship with Jesus or hinder you in your spiritual growth. Choose your inner circle of friends carefully. Many people have committed their lives to Jesus only to be detoured from their faith by the wrong "friends." Don't let that happen to you.

To grow as a Christian, you may need to change some of your closest friends. This doesn't mean that you stop loving or caring for them. It just means that you may not be able to have the same kind of relationship with them that you had before you gave your life to Christ. Know that if you have to give up some friends to follow Jesus, it's worth it. Also remember, God will give you new friends that share your faith and new values.

Make lifestyle and habit changes based on guidance from God's Word.

You're a new person in Christ. Your life is different now. The way you live should show it. This means that some old habits need to change. Places you go, things you say, things you do, the media you expose yourself to—your whole lifestyle now needs to reflect your commitment to Jesus. All of this is part of spiritual growth.

We make these changes, not because of a set of religious rules, but because we want to please and obey God. Living by His commands always means a better life for us.

The good news is that God will help you make these changes. When you decide to live as a Jesus follower, God will give you the power to do it. When temptation comes knocking at your door, learn to say NO! He'll help you!

> 1 Corinthians 10:13 (TLB)
> But remember this—the wrong desires that come into your life aren't anything new and

different. Many others have faced exactly the same problems before you. And no temptation is irresistible. You can trust God to keep the temptation from becoming so strong that you can't stand up against it, for he has promised this and will do what he says. He will show you how to escape temptation's power so that you can bear up patiently against it.

Live to honor God. Regularly ask yourself the question, "What would Jesus do?" Ask yourself, "What does the Bible say about this?" This will help you make better decisions that will lead you to a better life.

Become an active part of a Bible-believing, Bible-teaching church.

The Christian life was never intended to be lived alone. When you invited Jesus into your life, God brought you into His family. He wants you to be connected to other believers. You need them and they need you!

God's family is found in His church. To grow as a

follower of Jesus, you need to be a part of a church family. This is where believers worship, learn and serve together.

It's how we connect and cooperate with one another. It's also where we work together to reach others who need to know and experience God's love.

> Psalm 92:13 (NIV)
> Planted in the house of the Lord, they will flourish in the courts of our God.

> Hebrews 10:25 (NLT)
> And let us not neglect our meeting together, as some people do, but encourage one another, especially now that the day of his return is drawing near.

Become a committed, active part of a church. While no church is perfect, you should prayerfully choose a church that's focused on Jesus, that believes and teaches the Bible, and that reaches out with God's love to their community and the world. Look for signs of unity and harmony among the church family. Find a healthy church where you can grow and give, then jump in enthusiastically and be a part!

Participate in your church's groups and classes that will help you grow.

God uses other people to help you grow. Small Bible study, sharing and serving groups in your church are some of the best ways to meet other believers and build supportive friendships. Connecting with others in the church is one way God heals and matures you.

In these groups you talk about the Bible and pray together. You encourage each other. You work together. You help one another in practical ways. You grow together. Learn all you can and apply it in your life.

There may also be support groups and classes that can help you in practical areas like handling your finances, overcoming grief, growing your parenting skills and recovering from addictions.

Take advantage of all the resources available in your church that will move you forward in your spiritual development.

Put God first in your time, with your resources and talents.

The use of your time, talents and treasures matters to God. He wants you to make the most of all that He's given to you.

Remember that all of your resources ultimately come from God and belong to Him. As His follower, you now want to put Him first and handle them His way. Ask God to show you how to obey Him in these areas. You'll be blessed as you do!

Learn and believe God's promises for your life.

God has given you wonderful promises. They comfort, encourage and strengthen you. Here are just a few promises from God that will help you in your journey with Jesus:

- You have been forgiven.
  Ephesians 1:7 (NLT)
  He is so rich in kindness and grace that he purchased our freedom with the blood of his Son and forgave our sins.

  1 John 1:9 (NLT)
  But if we confess our sins to him, he is faithful and just to forgive us our sins and to cleanse us from all wickedness.

- You have been made right with God and have peace with Him.
  Romans 5:1 (NLT)
  Therefore, since we have been made right in God's sight by faith, we have peace with God because of what Jesus Christ our Lord has done for us.

- You have a brand-new life in Christ.
  2 Corinthians 5:17 (NLT)
  This means that anyone who belongs to Christ has become a new person. The old life is gone; a new life has begun!

- You have the Holy Spirit living in you.

Romans 8:10, 11 (NLT)
The Spirit gives you life because you have
been made right with God. The Spirit of
God, who raised Jesus from the dead, lives
in you.

- You have eternal life.
  1 John 5:13 (NIV)
  I write these things to you who believe in
  the name of the Son of God so that you
  may know that you have eternal life.

God is trustworthy. When He promises something,
you can count on it! These promises help you when
you believe them and trust them.

For example, if you don't feel like you're forgiven
because of something you've done wrong, hold on
to this promise:

1 John 1:9 (NLT)
But if we confess our sins to him, he is faithful
and just to forgive us our sins and to cleanse us
from all wickedness.

Let God's promises be stronger than your emotions. When you do, your emotions will eventually change.

Your decision to give your life to Jesus Christ is the greatest, wisest decision you'll ever make. Give Him your all. Get busy growing. Don't give up in the hard times. Your best days are ahead!

> Jeremiah 29:11-13 (NIV)
> "For I know the plans I have for you," declares the Lord, "plans to prosper you and not to harm you, plans to give you hope and a future. Then you will call on me and come and pray to me, and I will listen to you. You will seek me and find me when you seek me with all your heart."

> Philippians 1:6 (NLT)
> And I am certain that God, who began the good work within you, will continue his work until it is finally finished on the day when Christ Jesus returns.

Always remember that God loves you. He is for you. He will help you. Get to know Him. Learn to trust Him. Always obey Him and you'll experience blessings you can't imagine.

My husband and I started to see our lives change as we took steps to get involved at church, and we've become passionate about leading groups for married couples because of the impact being part of a small group has made in our family.

— Veronica

The Christian life
was never intended
to be lived alone.

Chapter 4

31-Day Devotional

The Bible is full of the truth we need to live wisely and well. This section will help you get started reading the Bible daily as you spend 31 days mining truths in bite-sized daily nuggets. The brief devotional thoughts will encourage you to find fresh insights in God's Word and live with a renewed sense of purpose and passion for Christ. Use the space provided to start journaling your journey by writing down your thoughts and insights.

Let's get growing!

Day 1
Getting It Right

If you declare with your mouth, "Jesus is Lord,"
and believe in your heart that God raised him from
the dead, you will be saved. For it is with your
heart that you believe and are justified, and it is
with your mouth that you profess your faith and
are saved. ROMANS 10:9, 10 NIV

Religion doesn't get people to heaven. We are saved
through a personal relationship with God by faith
in His Son, Jesus Christ. Making Jesus Christ the
Lord of your life is something you must do for
yourself. No one else can do this for you. You do it
by sincerely declaring from your heart to God and
to others your faith in Jesus as the Savior who died
for your sins and rose from the grave. If you have
not done this, do it today!

_____

_____

_____

_____

_____

_____

Day 2
Going Public

We were therefore buried with him through baptism into death in order that, just as Christ was raised from the dead through the glory of the Father, we too may live a new life. ROMANS 6:4 NIV

Going public with a commitment is a powerful moment. It's a declaration to the world that you mean business. It's putting yourself in front of others and saying, "This is real!" That's what water baptism is all about. It declares to the world that you have committed your life to Christ. It's powerful. It's important. If you have not been baptized as a believer in Jesus, go ahead and take the plunge!

_____

_____

_____

_____

_____

_____

_____

_____

Day 3
Price Paid

In him we have redemption through his blood, the
forgiveness of sins, in accordance with the riches of
God's grace. EPHESIANS 1:7 NIV

Redemption means to buy back. Because we're
sinners—people who reject God's Word and will
and substitute "I" where God should be—we owe
Him a debt. Just like a convicted criminal owes a
debt to society, we owe a debt to God. Jesus came
and gave His lifeblood in payment for the debt we
owe God. He bought us back! Aren't you glad to be
redeemed by His grace?

_____

_____

_____

_____

_____

_____

_____

_____

_____

Day 4
No Worries

Don't worry about anything; instead, pray about everything. Tell God what you need and thank him for all he has done. Then you will experience God's peace, which exceeds anything we can understand. His peace will guard your hearts and minds as you live in Christ Jesus. PHILIPPIANS 4:6, 7 NLT

Do you have a worry list? Of course, you do. We all do. Most probably there are things you're worried about right now. Your anxieties are robbing your peace and draining your emotional reserves. What are we supposed to do with our worries? The Bible gives us the answer. We are to turn our worry list into our prayer list. We are told to give our cares to God—all of them—and let Him handle them. It's an exchange program—our problems for His peace. Sounds great to me!

_____

_____

_____

_____

_____

Day 5
Yes, He Will

So let us come boldly to the throne of our gracious
God. There we will receive his mercy, and we
will find grace to help us when we need it most.
HEBREWS 4:16 NLT

When you need help it's great to have someone
to call on. It's especially wonderful to have a
relationship with someone who has promised their
availability and assistance to you before a crisis
arrives. Their advance promise of help gives you
confidence to reach out to them when you need
them. God has done this for you. Before your time
of need arrives, God has promised to help you.
When the hard times come, confidently take Him
up on His offer.

_____

_____

_____

_____

_____

_____

_____

Day 6
Grace That Works

For it was only through this wonderful grace that we believed in him. Nothing we did could ever earn this salvation, for it was the gracious gift from God that brought us to Christ! So no one will ever be able to boast, for salvation is never a reward for good works or human striving. We have become his poetry, a re-created people that will fulfill the destiny he has given each of us, for we are joined to Jesus, the Anointed One. Even before we were born, God planned in advance our destiny and the good works we would do to fulfill it!

Ephesians 2:8-10 TPT

The greatest gift we can receive is salvation—having our sins forgiven and receiving eternal life in God's presence. Jesus made this possible by what He did for us on the cross. When we accept His work, we receive His grace. We can't be good enough to get it. It's graciously and freely given when we put our faith in Jesus. And once we have received it, the same grace that saves us empowers us to do God's work in our world.

_____

_____

Day 7
Faith Food

So faith comes from hearing, that is, hearing the
Good News about Christ. ROMANS 10:17 NLT

Do you want stronger faith? You have to eat the
right spiritual food. When you regularly feed on
God's Word something supernatural happens:
Your faith muscles grow and your spiritual energy
increases. Take personal time every day to read
your Bible. Take time every week to study God's
Word with God's people. You'll be amazed at what
happens to your faith.

_____

_____

_____

_____

_____

_____

_____

_____

_____

_____

Day 8
Better Together

We must also consider how to encourage each other to show love and to do good things. We should not stop gathering together with other believers, as some of you are doing. Instead, we must continue to encourage each other even more as we see the day of the Lord coming.

HEBREWS 10:24, 25 GW

No matter how strong you are, you still need others—especially in your spiritual journey. You need to be encouraged, taught, prayed for and lovingly challenged by the example and words of other believers. That's what church is all about. You need the church, and the church needs you. Make it a priority.

_____

_____

_____

_____

_____

_____

_____

Day 9
Wise Up

Fear of the Lord is the foundation of wisdom.
Knowledge of the Holy One results in good
judgment. Wisdom will multiply your days and add
years to your life. If you become wise, you will be
the one to benefit. If you scorn wisdom, you will be
the one to suffer. PROVERBS 9:10-12 NLT

Fear is usually considered a bad thing. It's
something people work hard to overcome. Yet the
Bible tells us that a certain kind of fear is healthy,
good and the starting point for becoming a wise
person. We are told to "fear the Lord." What's this
all about? Fearing God means reverencing God's
wisdom and authority so much that you take His
word as the final word for your life. When this is
your attitude you are in the right position to learn
lessons from God that will make your life the best
it can be.

_____

_____

_____

_____

_____

Day 10
Mind Change

Don't copy the behavior and customs of this world,
but let God transform you into a new person by
changing the way you think. Then you will learn
to know God's will for you, which is good and
pleasing and perfect. ROMANS 12:2 NLT

It has been called "stinking thinking," and
everybody has it. It's that messed up way we
have of looking at God, other people and even at
ourselves that is twisted, distorted, painful and
unloving. It's the bad thinking that causes us to do
things, then ask ourselves, "What in the world was
I thinking?" God wants to change your mind. As
you get to know God's perspective and principles
you start viewing people and situations in a
healthier and holier way. You think better thoughts
and better thinking always leads to better decisions.

_____

_____

_____

_____

_____

Day 11
What's Great

Jesus answered him, "Love the Lord your God with
all your heart, with all your soul, and with all your
mind." This is the greatest and most important
commandment. The second is like it: "Love your
neighbor as you love yourself."
MATTHEW 22:37-39 GW

What is important to you? There's a simple way
to know. Honestly look at where you spend your
time, energy and money. What do you think about
most when you are choosing what you get to
think about? Unfortunately, when we are truthful
about the things occupying our attention, we often
discover that our focus is on stuff that doesn't
really matter. How easy it is to ignore what's really
important—loving God and loving others. Jesus
taught us that this is what real life is all about.

_____

_____

_____

_____

_____

Day 12
Favored

For the Lord God is brighter than the brilliance of a
sunrise! Wrapping himself around me like a shield,
he is so generous with his gifts of grace and glory.
Those who walk along his paths with integrity will
never lack one thing they need, for he provides it
all! PSALM 84:11 TPT

Bestowed favor. What a promise! Favor is
something someone does for you because they
know and love you. Favor opens a door of blessing
and opportunity you could not have opened
for yourself. It is a benefit that comes out of
relationship. Favor flows from the generosity and
goodness of a giver to an undeserving recipient.
God has favor to bestow on you. Why? Just
because He is good and generous, and He loves
you. Watch for His favor.

_____

_____

_____

_____

_____

Day 13
Little Things

The one who manages the little he has been given with faithfulness and integrity will be promoted and trusted with greater responsibilities. But those who cheat with the little they have been given will not be considered trustworthy to receive more.

LUKE 16:10 TPT

There is a little phrase that is often repeated: "Don't sweat the small stuff." Whoever coined this must have missed one of Jesus' lessons. He told us that how someone handles small things is one of the primary tests of a person's character. What we do with our little bit predicts what we'll do with a lot. According to Jesus, if we would learn to be faithful with the minuscule, we would be trusted with much more. If we handle the minors well, we'll be prepared for the majors.

_____

_____

_____

_____

_____

Day 14
Under Control

For the grace of God has appeared that offers salvation to all people. It teaches us to say "No" to ungodliness and worldly passions, and to live self-controlled, upright and godly lives in this present age. TITUS 2:11, 12 NIV

Most of us don't mind telling other people what to do. We're quick to pontificate our opinions, give our advice and offer our suggestions. We're experts at trying to control and change others and you have likely observed that few people pay much attention to your efforts. Here's a suggestion. Forget about controlling and changing others and start with yourself. Practice self-control.

_____

_____

_____

_____

_____

_____

Day 15
New You

Throw off your old sinful nature and your former way of life, which is corrupted by lust and deception. Instead, let the Spirit renew your thoughts and attitudes. Put on your new nature, created to be like God—truly righteous and holy.
Ephesians 4:22-24 NLT

History is divided into two parts: B.C. (Before Christ) and A.D. (from the Latin Anno Domini, "In the year of our Lord"). As a Christian, you have a B.C. and A.D. life. There's the person you were before you met Jesus and the person you now are after coming to know the Lord Jesus Christ. Make sure you're living in a way that reflects your A.D. life rather than your B.C. life!

_____

_____

_____

_____

_____

_____

Day 16
Roots

Rejoice in our confident hope. Be patient in trouble,
and keep on praying. ROMANS 12:12 NLT

In a hurricane, trees that have the strongest,
healthiest and deepest roots survive. The wind and
rain can't destroy them. They are grounded. Storms
are a part of life. We face financial storms, marital
storms, employment storms and physical storms.
What's the difference between those who survive
and those who don't? Spiritual roots that are
strong, healthy and deep. How is your root system?

_____

_____

_____

_____

_____

_____

_____

_____

_____

Day 17
Put Together

As God's obedient children, never again shape your lives by the desires that you followed when you didn't know better. Instead, shape your lives to become like the Holy One who called you. For Scripture says: "You are to be holy, because I am holy." 1 PETER 1:14-16 TPT

What does the word "holy" mean to you? People have lots of strange ideas about what it means to be holy. According to the Bible, to be holy is to be whole. It is to have the sinful and shattered places and pieces of your life put together by God. And when you are made whole by God, you want to love and obey Him wholly—you want to be holy.

_____

_____

_____

_____

_____

_____

_____

Day 18
Something Better

"For I know the plans I have for you," declares the
Lord, "plans to prosper you and not to harm you,
plans to give you hope and a future."
JEREMIAH 29:11 NIV

Everybody needs hope. You can't make it far in life
without it. Hope comes from the assurance that
something better is ahead, something promising
and purposeful. When you give yourself to God,
you open your life to hope. When you follow God,
there's always something good ahead for you.

_____

_____

_____

_____

_____

_____

_____

_____

_____

_____

Day 19
Let Go

Be kind and compassionate to one another,
forgiving each other, just as in Christ God forgave
you. EPHESIANS 4:32 NIV

When someone hurts you, it's likely that you want
them to hurt in return. Payback for pain is part
of the world's way of thinking. God calls us to do
things differently. When people create heartaches
for you, remember all the heartache you've caused
God. Remember the many times He's forgiven you.
Give other people the same grace God has given
you.

_____

_____

_____

_____

_____

_____

_____

_____

Day 20
This Is War

Put on all the armor that God supplies. In this way
you can take a stand against the devil's strategies.
This is not a wrestling match against a human
opponent. We are wrestling with rulers, authorities,
the powers who govern this world of darkness, and
spiritual forces that control evil in the heavenly
world. Ephesians 6:11, 12 GW

No wise and trained soldier goes into battle
without the proper equipment. Winning a war
requires the right resources. As Christians, we are
in a war with the spirits of darkness. It's a real war
with real casualties. Don't take it lightly. Dress
appropriately for your spiritual battle.

_____

_____

_____

_____

_____

_____

_____

Day 21
Not About Me

You are to lead by a different model. If you want to
be the greatest one, then live as one called to serve
others. The path to promotion and prominence
comes by having the heart of a bond-slave who
serves everyone. For even the Son of Man did not
come expecting to be served by everyone, but to
serve everyone, and to give his life as the ransom
price in exchange for the salvation of many.

MARK 10:43-45 TPT

Most of us have three favorite people in our
lives—me, myself and I. Don't believe it? Listen to
your words and watch your actions. Honest self-
observation usually confirms that we are highly
concerned about getting what we want, when we
want it, in the way we want it. Jesus taught and
modeled something different. He reminded us that
truly great people look for what they can give, not
get, and where they can serve, not be served.

_____

_____

_____

_____

Day 22
The Value of Everyone

You made all the delicate, inner parts of my body
and knit them together in my mother's womb.
Thank you for making me so wonderfully complex!
It is amazing to think about. Your workmanship is
marvelous—and how well I know it.
PSALM 139:13, 14 TLB

Life is precious. Life is holy. Life is a gift. Life is
from God. From the moment of conception, God's
great miracle called life declares His glory and
goodness. Value what God values. Honor what
God honors. Celebrate life!

_____

_____

_____

_____

_____

_____

_____

_____

Day 23
Power Aid

But you will receive power when the Holy Spirit
comes upon you. And you will be my witnesses,
telling people about me everywhere—in Jerusalem,
throughout Judea, in Samaria, and to the ends of
the earth. ACTS 1:8 NLT

"I can't" is a phrase that keeps lots of people
from doing good things and reaching their highest
potential. It's a disqualifying statement. Successfully
sharing Jesus with others is something we can't
do ourselves. Without God's help all our efforts to
reach people for Christ will be useless. The good
news is that God gave us a promise of power.
He promised the power of the Holy Spirit to do
through us what we can't do ourselves. When we
ask Him to fill us with the Holy Spirit, He answers.
He qualifies and empowers us to do His work.

_____

_____

_____

_____

_____

Day 24
Worth It

And as I watched, all of them were singing with
thunderous voices:
"Worthy is Christ the Lamb who was slaughtered
to receive great power and might, wealth and
wisdom, and honor, glory, and praise!"
REVELATION 5:12 TPT

What are your most valuable possessions? Your
list may include jewelry, your financial portfolio,
a collection of artwork or perhaps some family
heirloom. This is how we measure worth on earth.
Heaven measures it differently. The most valuable
and worthy thing in heaven isn't a thing–it's a
person, Jesus Christ, the Lamb of God. Our lives
significantly change for the better when we accept
heaven's definition of worth and give Jesus the
worth He deserves.

_____

_____

_____

_____

_____

Day 25
Grow Up!

We announce the message about Christ, and we use all our wisdom to warn and teach everyone, so that all of Christ's followers will grow and become mature. COLOSSIANS 1:28 CEV

Do you know someone that refuses to act their age? Our thoughts about them scream, "Grow up!" Some folks never grow up in their walk with God. They have known Jesus for years but still act like spiritual children. They are high-maintenance believers, continually needing spiritual pampering. They have not yet accepted responsibility to mature. Don't let this be you. To get going with God, you have to get growing with God.

_____

_____

_____

_____

_____

_____

_____

Day 26
Say What?

Your words are so powerful that they will kill or give life, and the talkative person will reap the consequences. PROVERBS 18:21 TPT

Your words change things. They can add or subtract strength. They win friends and build peace or create strife and generate division. They can inspire hope or kill it. What you say matters. Taming your tongue is tough, but it's worth the effort. Think before you speak.

_____

_____

_____

_____

_____

_____

_____

_____

_____

_____

Day 27
Upside Down

Don't be selfish; don't live to make a good impression on others. Be humble, thinking of others as better than yourself. Don't just think about your own affairs, but be interested in others, too, and in what they are doing. PHILIPPIANS 2:3, 4 TLB

"What is in it for me?" This question says a lot about a person's heart. It says something about what's really important to them. It exalts personal wants, plans and advantages. It causes people to make bad decisions that often hurt others. The key to a joyous life is the ability to consider others' desires and needs as carefully as you consider your own. When you think this way, it improves the direction your life takes and the impact you make on the people around you.

_____

_____

_____

_____

_____

_____

Day 28
Let God

Come to me, all who are tired from carrying heavy loads, and I will give you rest. Place my yoke over your shoulders, and learn from me, because I am gentle and humble. Then you will find rest for yourselves because my yoke is easy and my burden is light. MATTHEW 11:28-30 GW

Is your soul tired? Spiritual and emotional fatigue is the deepest kind of tiredness you will ever experience. It requires a supernatural fix. Jesus offers the cure. He invites you to come and release all your burdens to Him. Unload your cares on Jesus. Trust Him with all the things that concern you, and you will find the rest only He can give.

_____

_____

_____

_____

_____

_____

_____

Day 29
Making the Most

So be careful how you act; these are difficult days.
Don't be fools; be wise: make the most of every
opportunity you have for doing good.
EPHESIANS 5:15, 16 TLB

Every day we are all given the same gift, twenty-
four hours. No one gets more or less. You have
as much time as everyone else. Have you noticed
how some people get more done with their time
than others? Why? They make time count. They
don't waste it; they invest it. They look for the
opportunities in the moments. When we do this, the
Bible calls us wise.

_____

_____

_____

_____

_____

_____

_____

_____

Day 30
Taming a Tiger

But don't let the passion of your emotions lead
you to sin! Don't let anger control you or be fuel
for revenge, not for even a day. Don't give the
slanderous accuser, the Devil, an opportunity to
manipulate you! EPHESIANS 4:26, 27 TPT

Anger is one letter away from danger. What turns
anger to danger? A bad decision. What you decide
to do with your anger determines how it affects
you and others around you. You can handle it
productively and respond to people and situations
graciously, or you can become resentful, bitter and
vicious. The choice is yours. The consequences are
yours too.

_____

_____

_____

_____

_____

_____

_____

Day 31
Lane Makers

Therefore, since we are surrounded by such a huge
crowd of witnesses to the life of faith, let us strip
off every weight that slows us down, especially the
sin that so easily trips us up. And let us run with
endurance the race God has set before us.
HEBREWS 12:1 NLT

Racers are assigned lanes. Each runner's lane is
clearly marked. When the runner pays too much
attention to the lanes of other runners, she is
distracted. When she moves outside her assigned
lane, she's disqualified. God has given you a
life lane to run in. Stop comparing your lane to
someone else's. Stay in the lane God has marked for
your life. You will be happier, healthier and much
more fruitful.

_____

_____

_____

_____

_____

_____

*I have the privilege to give back
and live in obedience to the Lord,
and He never fails to meet all my needs
and bless my life as I serve Him.*

— Abeselom

Jeremiah 29:11-13 NIV

"For I know the plans I have for you," declares the Lord, "plans to prosper you and not to harm you, plans to give you hope and a future. Then you will call on me and come and pray to me, and I will listen to you. You will seek me and find me when you seek me with all your heart."

Chapter 5
Praying Scriptures Over Your Life

The following Bible verses will help you learn how to pray God's Word with confidence. Use them as you face different needs in your life. We encourage you to even memorize some of them. This will help you to continue growing as you renew your thinking in God's truth.

The Power of Prayer

Matthew 6:9-13 (NIV)
This, then, is how you should pray: "Our Father in heaven, hallowed be your name, your kingdom come, your will be done, on earth as it is in heaven. Give us today our daily bread. And forgive us our debts, as we also have forgiven our debtors. And lead us not into temptation, but deliver us from the evil one."

Matthew 7:7, 8 (NIV)
Ask and it will be given to you; seek and you will find; knock and the door will be opened to you. For everyone who asks receives; the one who seeks finds; and to the one who knocks, the door will be opened.

Mark 11:24 (NIV)
Therefore I tell you, whatever you ask for in prayer, believe that you have received it, and it will be yours.

Philippians 4:6, 7 (NLT)
Don't worry about anything; instead, pray about

everything. Tell God what you need, and thank him for all he has done. Then you will experience God's peace, which exceeds anything we can understand. His peace will guard your hearts and minds as you live in Christ Jesus.

Faith

Mark 9:23, 24 (TPT)
Jesus said to him, "What do you mean 'if'? If you are able to believe, all things are possible to the believer." When he heard this, the boy's father cried out with tears, saying, "I do believe, Lord; help my little faith!"

Romans 10:17 (NIV)
Consequently, faith comes from hearing the message, and the message is heard through the word about Christ.

Ephesians 2:8, 9 (NLT)
God saved you by his grace when you believed. And you can't take credit for this; it is a gift from God. Salvation is not a reward for the good things we have done, so none of us can boast about it.

Hebrews 11:1 (NLT)
Faith is the confidence that what we hope for will
actually happen; it gives us assurance about things
we cannot see.

1 John 5:14 (NIV)
This is the confidence we have in approaching God:
that if we ask anything according to his will, he
hears us.

Healing in Your Body, Mind and Emotions

Psalm 23:1-4 (NIV)
The Lord is my shepherd, I lack nothing. He makes
me lie down in green pastures, he leads me beside
quiet waters, he refreshes my soul. He guides me
along the right paths for his name's sake.
Even though I walk through the darkest valley, I
will fear no evil, for you are with me; your rod and
your staff, they comfort me.

Psalm 103:1-5 (NIV)
Praise the Lord, my soul; all my inmost being, praise
his holy name. Praise the Lord, my soul, and forget
not all his benefits—who forgives all your sins and

heals all your diseases, who redeems your life from the pit and crowns you with love and compassion, who satisfies your desires with good things so that your youth is renewed like the eagle's.

Psalm 107:20 (NIV)
He sent out his word and healed them; he rescued them from the grave.

Isaiah 53:4, 5 (NLT)
Yet it was our weaknesses he carried; it was our sorrows that weighed him down. And we thought his troubles were a punishment from God, a punishment for his own sins! But he was pierced for our rebellion, crushed for our sins. He was beaten so we could be whole. He was whipped so we could be healed.

Matthew 8:16, 17 (NLT)
That evening many demon-possessed people were brought to Jesus. He cast out the evil spirits with a simple command, and he healed all the sick. This fulfilled the word of the Lord through the prophet Isaiah, who said, "He took our sicknesses and removed our diseases."

Matthew 9:35 (NLT)
Jesus traveled through all the towns and villages
of that area, teaching in the synagogues and
announcing the Good News about the Kingdom.
And he healed every kind of disease and illness.

Matthew 10:1 (NLT)
Jesus called his twelve disciples together and gave
them authority to cast out evil spirits and to heal
every kind of disease and illness.

John 16:33 (NIV)
I have told you these things, so that in me you may
have peace. In this world you will have trouble. But
take heart! I have overcome the world.

Romans 12:1, 2 (NIV)
Therefore, I urge you, brothers and sisters, in view
of God's mercy, to offer your bodies as a living
sacrifice, holy and pleasing to God—this is your
true and proper worship. Do not conform to the
pattern of this world, but be transformed by the
renewing of your mind. Then you will be able to
test and approve what God's will is—his good,
pleasing and perfect will.

Ephesians 4:26, 27 (NLT)
And "don't sin by letting anger control you." Don't
let the sun go down while you are still angry, for
anger gives a foothold to the devil.

Philippians 4:8 (NLT)
And now, dear brothers and sisters, one final thing.
Fix your thoughts on what is true, and honorable,
and right, and pure, and lovely, and admirable.
Think about things that are excellent and worthy
of praise.

2 Timothy 1:7 (NLT)
For God has not given us a spirit of fear and
timidity, but of power, love, and self-discipline.

James 5:13-16 (NIV)
Is anyone among you in trouble? Let them pray.
Is anyone happy? Let them sing songs of praise. Is
anyone among you sick? Let them call the elders of
the church to pray over them and anoint them with
oil in the name of the Lord. And the prayer offered
in faith will make the sick person well; the Lord
will raise them up. If they have sinned, they will be
forgiven. Therefore confess your sins to each other

and pray for each other so that you may be healed. The prayer of a righteous person is powerful and effective.

1 John 4:4 (NLT)
But you belong to God, my dear children. You have already won a victory over those people, because the Spirit who lives in you is greater than the spirit who lives in the world.

Giving and Financial Provision

Malachi 3:10-12 (NLT)
"Bring all the tithes into the storehouse so there will be enough food in my Temple. If you do," says the Lord of Heaven's Armies, "I will open the windows of heaven for you. I will pour out a blessing so great you won't have enough room to take it in! Try it! Put me to the test! Your crops will be abundant, for I will guard them from insects and disease. Your grapes will not fall from the vine before they are ripe," says the Lord of Heaven's Armies. "Then all nations will call you blessed, for your land will be such a delight," says the Lord of Heaven's Armies.

Matthew 6:19-21 (NLT)
Don't store up treasures here on earth, where moths eat them and rust destroys them, and where thieves break in and steal. Store your treasures in heaven, where moths and rust cannot destroy, and thieves do not break in and steal. Wherever your treasure is, there the desires of your heart will also be.

Matthew 6:33 (NIV)
But seek first his kingdom and his righteousness, and all these things will be given to you as well.

Luke 6:38 (NIV)
Give, and it will be given to you. A good measure, pressed down, shaken together and running over, will be poured into your lap. For with the measure you use, it will be measured to you.

Philippians 4:12, 13 (NIV)
I know what it is to be in need, and I know what it is to have plenty. I have learned the secret of being content in any and every situation, whether well fed or hungry, whether living in plenty or in want. I can do all this through him who gives me strength.

Philippians 4:19 (NIV)
And my God will meet all your needs according to
the riches of his glory in Christ Jesus.

1 Timothy 6:6-10 (NIV)
But godliness with contentment is great gain. For
we brought nothing into the world, and we can
take nothing out of it. But if we have food and
clothing, we will be content with that. Those who
want to get rich fall into temptation and a trap and
into many foolish and harmful desires that plunge
people into ruin and destruction. For the love of
money is a root of all kinds of evil. Some people,
eager for money, have wandered from the faith and
pierced themselves with many griefs.

1 Timothy 6:17-19 (NLT)
Teach those who are rich in this world not to be
proud and not to trust in their money, which is
so unreliable. Their trust should be in God, who
richly gives us all we need for our enjoyment. Tell
them to use their money to do good. They should
be rich in good works and generous to those in
need, always being ready to share with others. By
doing this they will be storing up their treasure as

a good foundation for the future so that they may experience true life.

Salvation for Family Members and Others

Acts 16:31-34 (NIV)
They replied, "Believe in the Lord Jesus, and you will be saved—you and your household." Then they spoke the word of the Lord to him and to all the others in his house. At that hour of the night the jailer took them and washed their wounds; then immediately he and all his household were baptized. The jailer brought them into his house and set a meal before them; he was filled with joy because he had come to believe in God—he and his whole household.

Romans 10:13 (NIV)
For, "Everyone who calls on the name of the Lord will be saved."

1 Timothy 2:4 (GW)
He wants all people to be saved and to learn the truth.

2 Peter 3:9 (NLT)
The Lord isn't really being slow about his promise,
as some people think. No, he is being patient
for your sake. He does not want anyone to be
destroyed, but wants everyone to repent.

Relationships

Proverbs 17:17 (TPT)
A dear friend will love you no matter what, and a
family sticks together through all kinds of trouble.

Matthews 5:44 (TPT)
However, I say to you, love your enemy, bless the
one who curses you, do something wonderful for
the one who hates you, and respond to the very
ones who persecute you by praying for them.

Matthew 6:14, 15 (GW)
If you forgive the failures of others, your heavenly
Father will also forgive you. But if you don't
forgive others, your Father will not forgive your
failures.

Luke 14:11 (NLT)
For those who exalt themselves will be humbled,
and those who humble themselves will be exalted.

John 13:34 (TPT)
So I give you now a new commandment: Love each
other just as much as I have loved you.

Romans 15:7 (NIV)
Accept one another, then, just as Christ accepted
you, in order to bring praise to God.

Ephesians 4:31, 32 (NLT)
Get rid of all bitterness, rage, anger, harsh words,
and slander, as well as all types of evil behavior.
Instead, be kind to each other, tenderhearted,
forgiving one another, just as God through Christ
has forgiven you.

Philippians 2:3, 4 (NLT)
Don't be selfish; don't try to impress others.
Be humble, thinking of others as better than
yourselves. Don't look out only for your own
interests, but take an interest in others, too.

The Work of the Holy Spirit

Luke 11:13 (NIV)
If you then, though you are evil, know how to give good gifts to your children, how much more will your Father in heaven give the Holy Spirit to those who ask him!

Luke 24:49 (NLT)
And now I will send the Holy Spirit, just as my Father promised. But stay here in the city until the Holy Spirit comes and fills you with power from heaven.

John 14:25, 26 (GW)
I have told you this while I'm still with you. However, the helper, the Holy Spirit, whom the Father will send in my name, will teach you everything. He will remind you of everything that I have ever told you.

Acts 1:8 (NLT)
But you will receive power when the Holy Spirit comes upon you. And you will be my witnesses, telling people about me everywhere—in Jerusalem,

throughout Judea, in Samaria, and to the ends of the earth.

Galatians 5:22, 23 (NIV)
But the fruit of the Spirit is love, joy, peace, forbearance, kindness, goodness, faithfulness, gentleness and self-control. Against such things there is no law.

Ephesians 5:18, 19 (NLT)
Don't be drunk with wine, because that will ruin your life. Instead, be filled with the Holy Spirit, singing psalms and hymns and spiritual songs among yourselves, and making music to the Lord in your hearts.

About the Author

Dale A. O'Shields is the founder and Senior Pastor of Church of the Redeemer, a multi-cultural, multi-generational and multi-campus church in the greater Washington DC area. Pastor Dale is known for his relevant teaching style focused on the practical application of God's Word. His messages are broadcast widely through radio, television and online. His heart to equip and encourage pastors and church leaders has led him to be a key founder of the United Pastors Network and a frequent conference speaker. He has also written several books, devotionals and group study guides. Pastor Dale and his wife Terry have two married daughters and seven grandchildren.